ed

Peter Daniels

Smith/Doorstop Books

Published 1994 by
Smith/Doorstop Books
The Poetry Business
The Studio
Byram Arcade
Westgate
Huddersfield HD1 1ND

ISBN 1 869961 62 5
Typeset at The Poetry Business
Printed by Swiftprint, Huddersfield

The Poetry Business gratefully acknowledges the
help of Kirklees Metropolitan Council and Yorkshire
& Humberside Arts.

Acknowledgements
Thanks are due to the editors of the following publica-
tions, in which some of these poems have previously
appeared: *Foolscap, South West Competition 1993,* James
White Review, Verse, Sugar and Snails (Oscars), *Wilfred
Owen Association Competition* 1991, *The Independent,
Critical Quarterly, Take Any Train* (Oscars), *Of Eros and
Of Dust* (Oscars), *The North, Poetry London Newsletter,
Art and Understanding, Jugular Defences* (Oscars), *Lan-
guage of Water, The Rialto.*

CONTENTS

Peter Daniels grew up in Birmingham and has lived in London since 1982, working as a librarian and indexer. He edited *Take Any Train* (Oscars Press, 1990), an anthology of gay men's poetry, and two issues of the *James White Review*, Minneapolis. Recently he has become a joint editor of *Poetry London Newsletter*, and with Steve Anthony has co-edited *Jugular Defences: an AIDS anthology* for Oscars Press.

In 1991 he was winner of the Poetry Business Competition with Moniza Alvi. Their joint collection, *Peacock Luggage*, is available from us, price £4.95.

PICKUP

1.

Pick up the vibrations
       underneath the room,
the hum of celebration and the
       general conversation,
what this place needs
       is a broom, what
we could do with is a
       broomhandle, what we could
sweep up in a sweepstake
might pay the upkeep

2.

Pick up, dark at night, rainy,
       gutters gurgling
and taxis chugging over,
pick up a muscular piece of
       streetcorner wildlife, pick up
a man in a grey suit with a bulging
       briefcase, pick up a man
in a meter reader's uniform – contact:
       buzz, buzz, crackle –
the rain: splash, hiss, gurgle –
the chugchugchugchug slam roar away
       of the late night taxi

3.

Pick up a sweet nectarine, pick up
        a purple aubergine, pick up
a soft wrinkled carrot and a sockful of garlic,
pick up the old globe artichokes,
        pick up the new disposables,
pick up, wrap up and play with them,
make me a rainbow
        to moan about all day,
show me to the crock of gold,
then take it away

KINGS

The king of touch is good to fling with, waltzing from
ballroom to bedroom. Feel under his skin, the veins
his blood is roaring through.

> As everyone acknowledges, you can't leave people
> dancing on the edge of a cliff.

The king of tact knows a trick you don't,
but he holds his powers in reserve, his
is the unexpected gift.

> You can't insist on heroism, even
> when it does make sense.

The king of trust is aware what the night can be, and
he waits there, sparking and vulnerable, till he can
prick a hole in the dark.

> Now look what you've made me do.

The kings of truth have told you: People go, they die, they
won't be perfect. Don't wait up for your climbing joy.
Sweat is water, salt and grease.

> 'Take off that ridiculous gown' he says.

A CLOCKWORK UNCLE

All happy families are alike. But he ponders
the stupid pitfalls between them, crossing
over a plank bridge with his dog, to the path
      along the raw red lampposts, and the sun
      that pokes through the trees and chimneys.

They are alike because they are happy.
In his pocket, he weighs up how he can
wake his rusty uncle, the one with
      a heart that chimes underwater.
      Here boy, come out of there. Good dog.

Because they are alike, they are happy.
Back in the castle: 'Come here, it's time
to plump up your mother's pillow.'
      The Queen's hair folds over in
      grey blonde waves. She twists a ring.

If they are happy, they must have something
in common. Now, what if he puts a pea
under the mattress? Here is the brown plush
      uncle with the sausagey arms
      and a mechanical growl. Grrrr.

If they are that alike, are they happy
to be like that? The red-painted lampposts
have faded like geraniums. The dog
      isn't stupid, but doesn't know
      he doesn't know. Come out of there.

They are all rather similar. He's not happy
with this yet: is this a dream of Uncle
in a wig? in his ceremonial uniform?
      No, it's the Princess in pinstripes and a tie.
      With her legs it's a shame, but her choice.

Happiness is like a warm puppy, but a dog
is not a toy. Here boy, teatime, we're late.
Where's that ball? Back in the castle,
       jam tarts and golden honey.
       Discussing trains with his brother.

How they like to be happy! But he has no brother,
and Uncle needs mending. Upstairs he knows
there's a broom cupboard full of spare parts,
       old screws in tins, good heavy brass.
       The proverb is something musty.

They are happy because they are what they are.
The tool kit is not quite forbidden:
'I didn't think you'd be interested.'
       He doesn't know what to learn
       but Father probably knows best.

Happy the man who has his quiver full
like the giant in the book. The woods are
full of mushrooms, soft and dusty like
       Grandmother's featherbeds. The dog
       will die, but his pups will come again.

Happy thoughts, like 'Train set' or 'Walkies'
keep his hands busy, but boys become uncles and
back in his little bunk with the blankets tented
       it's probably too late. As they say,
       'You know where you are with a thing.'

Families happen whether or not you like it,
whatever you do. Let's pretend the Princess
is Queen of Tarts – but that's in another
       kingdom, the one where the hero
       comes dressed as a servant.

FAMILY

I'm getting used to the household here,
'informal', I think you said.
But who is the woman that brings rice puddings
and tucks you up in bed?

'I thought you might ask, and it's hard to explain,
but let me think this out:
she's my ex-lover's ex-lover's ex-lover's mother,
she likes to get out and about.'

On Tuesday I met with a man on the stairs,
he was holding up a length of pipe.
He ruffled his moustache as he gave me a smile
– do you think I'd be his type?

'That's my ex-lover's ex-lover's therapist's plumber,
he came to fix the U-bend and stayed.
He's always handy with his monkey wrench
but he's not to be had, I'm afraid.'

Who was the man that called last night?
When I told you, you grabbed at the phone.
He was obviously someone special to you
so I thought I'd leave you alone.

'He's my three-times-ex-lover's next lover's lover,
we go back quite a long way.
We may not ever have been that close
but we're family, I think you'd say.

'We've often bumped into each other in crowds
– once we met at a bus stop in Spain –
but he's dying now, at his parents' house.
I'll never see him again.'

INTERPLANETARY AND DOMESTIC

Out from two circling planets, Us and Them,
journeyed the daring Sappho expedition
parallel to the bold Uranian mission,
with our respective crews both butch and femme.

We, who converged on Earthlings with our aim
founding a Fairy Land or Lesbian Nation,
find that we have to share accommodation
though our domestic views are not the same.

Cramped in our style by straitened circumstances,
if we intend to maximise our chances,
bullshit and bitchery should come to terms;

we have to organise our kitchen-sharing,
open the cans and set about preparing
crazier salads for our dish of worms.

MR LARKIN

'This was Mr Larkin's room. He kept
the catalogue the whole time he was here
at Head Collection.' Emptied shelves, except
the older backlog; Urgent Books to Clear

dealt with on trolleys; on the Journals side
some loose-tied bundles. 'Mr Larkin took
our Abstracts section fully in his stride.'
Desk, swivel chair, wastepaper bin, no hook

behind the door, no room for pending trays.
They took me. So it happens now that I
grapple with what he organised, and gaze
out at the white-glazed courtyard bricks, and try

putting my mind to indexing, to feed
the glimmering screen he budgeted to buy;
and follow his encapsulating need
to find the keywords from the chaos – why

he kept on plugging at a hundred drawers
banked in their wooden frame, while at his desk
subject-arrangements for the world outdoors
helped him to place the mundane and grotesque.

But where the catalogue he built contains
his life, he sought no terms with broader scope
to shelter from defeating winds and rains
than hospitals, and death; refusing hope,

he gave the Toad, work, his imagination:
and how much more his love for it could show
than take the dry embrace of desperation
knowing he wanted better, I don't know.

EXCESSES OF THE PRIOR OF INCHCOLM

Deposed from office, 1224

A monk is illuminating
aspects of the deadlier sins.
The Prior is much in his mind.
The blue snake twined
round the capital of Pride
follows his long smooth shape.
Something of his in the smirk
of the Scarlet Whore.

The Prior does not inspect the work.
He strides freely, he is not afraid
of the hellfires they resentfully
score down for him. Along this road
he will elevate self and soul: to see
his priority shining out beyond
the stony shape of the cloistered island.

UTOPIA

Behind the beyond
a square is kept
sacred by the souls
of the pure symmetrists.

A perfectly swept
enclosure, fenced
with a simple chain-link
parallelogram.

The trees are cones.

The gardeners are conceptualists
who know a statue
when they think of one.

The slabs and lines
are theoretically exact.

The lamps
to light the spaciousness
are globes.

The dogs trot round the surfaces
illustrating parallax:
pyramids to flowerbeds,
flowerbeds to topiary.

The bushes are peacocks
mounted on cubes
to represent graciousness.

The terrace is concrete,
the vistas are infinite.

The flowers are intact
and their names are definite,
their roots in fact.

THE PHOENIX

He slipped away from his party
when something said to him:
why not be quiet and steamy? go where
the pomegranates have swollen to splitting,
and vases gorge with orchids and lilies.
Through the glass doors, their waxiness
gleams in the semi-dark.
The air soaks him in mould.

This is one way to look for it.
Listening to the closed-off music,
he has been standing still, finding it harder to breathe,
when over his shoulder
a bird wafts in.
Yes, there are scorch marks on that banana frond.
He is caught by this dry breeze.

He can clear his diary,
throw out the social functions
and lock the glassed-in jungle.
Christmas in the ruins
of a dried-mud castle.
What is it to be fertile?
Back there in the desert
the Phoenix has a nest ready.

BREAKFAST, PALERMO

One golden glazed bun, sliced open.
One scoop of custardy ice cream, speckled
with chips of fruit and chocolate.
Sandwich them lavishly.

To be eaten in uniform by a young soldier,
in one careless hand, espresso in the other.
At the chrome bar, more coffee is hissing.
Sunshine slants in early, yellow.
Not a speck on his trousers.

THE MORMONS IN SICILY

There's something I didn't mention, that time we stood
                    in the bus going to Monreale
watching the Mormons, noticing their badges – the
                    title Elder translated 'Anziano':
Anziano Norton, Anziano Schmitz, Anziano Miller,
                    and Anziano Bellini the local boy,
returning from Utah with his brethren to convert the
                    rest of the island,
perhaps including his mother. There was great zeal to
                    labour in the vineyard.

What I didn't say was: as the bus filled with people
                    and jolted uphill to the cathedral
a man, crowded in behind me, was jolting in a rhythm
                    that wasn't the bouncing suspension,
and for a good ten minutes was fucking me, without
                    actually fucking me, till the bus
came to his ordinary street and he got off as usual,
                    while we stayed on
to the end of the line, to enjoy the Norman masterpiece,
                    with the Latter-Day Saints.

NINETY SECONDS

To get to the edge, take
the Tornado roller-coaster,
not a bad way to get into trouble,
to wind you up on the way up and let you go
                                on the way round and
                                                    down
    into the bottom of inertia and   up the other side of
                                gravity
                            and twisting you
                                into the meaning of
                                    torque, and is there
compensation for the spin of the earth, those things you
never quite understood
                and maybe
        preferred not to –
you've got them now, you're in them, you always
                                        have been but here's the
                                                    rush
                                        that puts you to feeling
life might always be so much at once if you could
                            always feel it – they say
skydiving overcomes your fear of drowning – like taking
        California Highway One
edging the cliffs – and what if the big quake
                            happens when you're up here
    – only blocks away there's
                    the main street of Santa Cruz
                                still rebuilding, two

18

years later, and back in
San Francisco on the Bay Bridge they point out where a
woman drove into the sudden gap

　　　　　　　　and your glasses fall off
　　　　　　　　　　but
　　　　　　　you've caught them and you can't see
where you're being
　　　　　　　turned for the last
　　of the ride but by then
you know that
the slight ache you had in your knee

　　　　　　　　will have disappeared,
at least for the rest of the day.
　　　The　　rest　　of　　the　　day.
　　　The　　　　rest　　　　of　　the　　day.

FALL

for Carl Morse

This New England Fall, they say, so disappointing:
the damp summer. But for novice visitors it burns enough
in yellows; in a few red hollows there's a reliable
burst of swamp maples. The dead ones are sugar maples:
something is wrong, they have been wasting.

I've just been in Manhattan. Central Park has scarcely turned,
but 'Down East' maybe those rocky Maine forests are more
the true explosive colour. I'm trying to absorb
some of the American intensities. People say to me:
'I'm tired of New York' – meaning, 'Too many friends are dead.'

Over in a Chelsea brownstone, there's the glow of a hermit's cave.
He came back from Maine ten years ago, burning. His table
is spread, he chooses things for the light, the angle
of the shadow on the seventeenth floor: and still
whatever he can get said and done comes hot from within.

Once upon a time, he says, he went back to the woods: plain
furniture, his milltown background, chopping logs. Hardships
refine simplicities. There at home, he heard from the neighbours
and the local policeman. The way they saw it came down to
who wants this queer back anyway? So they brought their guns.

All along the Appalachian system, the volcanic intrusions,
the metamorphics, even in Manhattan: Central Park
shows the rocks that ancient heat and pressure made
solid enough to build New York. City of live and dead, gathered
where he can clang his bell and call his heretic psalm.

WALL STREET

We walk further downtown, beyond the Village graffiti
that says AIDS IS THRUSH
AND IT'S CURABLE!
Life is money and the buildings are bigger here.
It's Ash Wednesday,
this is a day to commemorate
some crisis: all the last-born, maybe,
picked from among the perfect suits, the ones
wearing on their groomed brows a smudge
like a smear of sex.
Look how ready they are,
it makes them hunger for six weeks without sin.

Being with my sacrilegious Manhattan friend,
it's time to look at a few spiky old churches,
because we don't visit here often.
Remarkable needlework: the white altarcloth, with
crossed pairs of three-tail scourges in red.
It seems, worrying rumours have started
about the condition of the body of Christ.
More smudges: gladly humble
to wear this dirt mark in public.
And Jesus, with his robes hanging off him,
stands at a bank of candles, warming his hands.

BIRMINGHAM

1st July 1992

The years of Indian meals, that hot summer of Saleem's:
I don't need to live here now, it's all inside me, even
the place of worship, where I've never been.
It's pouring rain, and they've altered all the buses.
On the curved inside wall of a Romanesque universe
a shepherd holds a lamb, saved for the sacrifice.

The priest only knew his last year. 'That's not
the Adrian we knew,' Anne says later, but
we meet as the gathered body of Adrian:
I've brought a wide-eyed medical student,
opening cupboards full of lubricant, finding out
languages, Leningrad tram routes, maps of everywhere.

– 'His Methodist upbringing gave him joy,
he found in the Catholic Church, peace.'
– 'He said to me once as we handed out
Gay Liberatlon leaflets in the Bull Ring –
we'd both of us grown up as Methodists –
It's just like going out witnessing, isn't it?'

Body of Adrian, we greet, bless, part with him
in these inexpert prayers: and as he rises
in floating voices and incense, we're sure
he'll be unafraid when one of the bearded saints
pulls him through the Oratory dome and into
the other side; unembarrassed, certainly.

In the hall behind, we gather for wine and gossip,
accounting for some of these years, and what
we are up to, our changes of shape and hair
and lovers; looking for Adrian, seemingly
missing his party; then back to the Ladypool Road
for one more indifferent curry, as ever.

CHAIN LETTER

With love all things are possible. *This paper has*
been sent to you for good luck.
                    Postmark Windsor.
My street name wrongly spelt, as always, no clue there.

It has been around the world 9 times. This luck has now
been sent to you — a poor xerox. Soon folk technology will
mailmerge, as in: 'Dear Mr PERIODICALS LIBRARIAN, you may
have already won a holiday'
                    but not yet.
                            You will receive
good luck within 4 days… Provided you in turn send it on.

Before leaving the house, I listen for today's
Cancer predictions: 'Friends may bother you.'
In the shop, the chocolate egg merchandising:
'Every fourth surprise is either Donald Duck
or another personality.'
                    Nothing has happened yet.
This is no joke.
Don't send money as fate has no pride
                            but it always
takes the credit, as a refusal often offends.

While in the Philippines, Gene Welch lost his wife 6 days after
receiving this letter. He failed to circulate the letter.
However before her death he received 7,755,000 dollars.

At the bus stop, we are all late. She growls: 'Oh no, I wish
I'd caught that other bus.' Transport is all bad luck
where I live.
            The chain comes from Venezuela… the copy must
tour the world…

                    I hurry to take another route, and catch my thumb

in the train door. Remember the day the escalator melted,
maybe they all could have climbed it, if they'd walked
around that ladder.

After a few days
you will get a surprise, this is true even if you are not
superstitious.

'Dear Valentine,

You may already have contracted
disease no. 8432A. Please take this card to your nearest clinic… '

A few days later he won a lottery of 2 million dollars.

The house will be crammed with omens. Electric bulbs
won't stop moonlight shining through the window.

She was plagued with various problems including
expensive car repairs.

Why did that dog bark at me? Victim.
The post could bring
anything.

'Dear Mr D,

When you read this you may be already
dead.' Misdirected. Wrong street.

She finally
typed the letter as promised and got a new car.

I get in to work. My pinched thumb is not badly hurt,
I wash it.

Send copies to people you think need good luck.
Luck has no loyalty. Do I need friends in Windsor?

Do not keep this letter. It must leave your hands
within 96 hours. Do not ignore this.

My own good 96 hours,
and I'll be listening

for when the music stops. Pass it on.

HUNGER

Eating has been leaving me hollow
for a man born creating
new appetites, raising desires, fucking
his home from home. He's finding
his way, always leaving
unfinished business: reaching
for more than one requiring
more of him. Watch him building
a naked art form, letting it lift. Gulping
it in. A need the size of Glasgow

but London-greedy. Yes, you. Mouth full of
native tongue, but you make yourself
understood. When it arises, we hold it
how it comes, how we like it. But it's
holding only a snatched handful of
days from a year and both of us
insatiable – better put it away. It's
getting impossible. Let's give it up.

I walk home cold at midnight, past the baker's:
breathe in the warm emotion of yeast
rousing a cloud of half-satisfied
hunger, creating itself.

BE PREPARED

When I caught him in the bar I didn't know him
till I saw his curious ring that was his mother's:
I'd erased his unlucky face, and thought it was
… somebody else. Glad I did the wrong thing,
still I left him there with my embarrassment.
> I keep a spare torch for him in the closet:
> the batteries are obsolete now, you can't get them.

Every good boy deserves favour, and that
includes me: doing unto others, doing good
by stealth, doing the vacuuming only when alone
because it isn't done to be seen working,
wanting to be a Wise Virgin. Ready when you are:
> till then I have man-sized tissues by my lamp
> and a flip-top bin to discharge them into.

If I were a qualified body electrician
I'd connect up our moments of weakness
and demonstrate how they point, they rub.
The hand, the screwdriver, the spark – we learn
insulation, and our fantasies wear condoms.
> There's a candle for you under the bed,
> come over and hide there some time.

Rubbing together like boy scouts can start up
blazes of inflammatory behaviour, every
lifesaving effort a worse liability.
I doubt if we'd manage the heart-shaped badge,
and I don't stay up reading the instruction manual.
> For you I've put an oil can in the garage
> and labelled it 'Danger'. You got a match?

No need to skin our desire, or clothe it with
tit bells to warn each other how to hurt.
Promise I won't write, if you won't read, and
I'll fix our weaknesses to glow without touching
till dawn comes up through a rubber window.

     I want a torch to hand on ahead of me.
     Go on: we shine from the sheer need of light.